A USER'S GUIDE TO MEN

An OPTIMA book
copyright © 1993 Alison Everitt
illustration copyright © 1993 Alison Everitt

First published by Optima in 1993

The right of the author has been asserted.

ISBN 0 356 21032 4

Typeset by The Guernsey Press Co. Ltd,
Guernsey, Channel Islands

Printed and bound in Great Britain by
The Guernsey Press Co. Ltd, Guernsey, Channel Islands

Optima
A Division of
Little, Brown and Company (UK) Limited
165 Great Dover Street
London SE1 4YA

Dedicated to any woman who has ever been interested in, enamoured of, or infected by those macho, mysterious marvels called MEN.

CONTENTS

4

THE AUTHOR . . .

ALISON EVERITT
Cartoonist. Writer.
TV Presenter and
MAN WATCHER.
(it's a tough job, but
someone's got to do it!)

Other books by the author . . .

Still available. Still Cheap.
(The books, that is!)

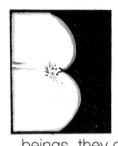efore you go any further, I have to say that there are some JOLLY NICE men about.
(I have to say that, or they'll make my life a misery.)
They can talk to us as equal, intelligent human beings, they can listen to our problems without trying to get a quick peek at our cleavages, and they can put up with us talking about our ovaries without passing out.
Unfortunately, the rest of their sex has a LOT of catching up to do, and this book is here to help you to sort the Romeos from the Rats, and the Supermen from the Slimeballs, as well as taking an in-depth look at what makes them tick, what makes them stray . . . and what makes them wear the same pair of jeans for the best part of a year? . . .

EVOLUTION . . .

The first man, depending on what you believe in, was either Adam or Guy the Gorilla. Women have come a long way since the days of being dragged around by the hair and chained to the cave over a hot mammoth steak. But what about men?

APE   NEANDERTHAL   PORNO PUBLISHER   TABLOID JOURNALIST   ESTATE AGENT

In particular, what about the man in your life? How far has *he* evolved?
Fill out the questionnaire at the back and find out!

MEN AND DOGS . . .

WHY DO MEN LIKE DOGS?

— Dogs give unquestioning love. You can swear at them, starve them, even beat them, and they'll still love you.

— Dogs like any attention you care to give them and don't have to be taken out to dinner before they're impressed with you.

— Dogs *don't* get headaches.

— Dogs don't nag them, spend their money, or ask them where they were last night.

— Dogs are stupid, and make *them* look smart.

11

Some men feel much more manly because their dogs look huge and tough.

Some men feel much more interesting because they dress their dogs to look trendy.

Some men just feel a complete twerp because their dogs belong to their wives.

Other men have dogs so they can pick up women . . .

. . . one way or another!

FETCH!

13

HOW ARE MEN SIMILAR TO DOGS?

— Both need an awful lot of attention.

— Both have extremely dodgy toilet habits.

— And if you look at them twice, both will follow you home.

WHY DO MEN *ENVY* DOGS?

— Dogs are free spirits.

— Dogs don't have to work.

— Dogs don't have to get married.

— Dogs can do what all men long to do . . . lick their own genitals . . .

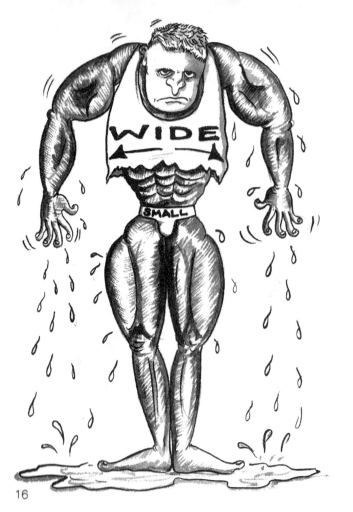

SPOT THE . . .

BODYBUILDER

Where You Find Him: On his way to or from the gym.

How To Spot Him: He's the one stuck in a doorway.

What started as a harmless twice a week trip to the gym soon becomes a real obsession, and before you know it, he's shaved off his chest hair, is permanently smothered in baby oil, and his arms can't touch his sides.

Advantages: You always feel safe when you're out with him.

Disadvantages: He'll eat you out of house and home, burst through any clothes you buy him, and you'll never be sure if it's passionate love-making, or just his evening work out!

. . . MARRIED MAN

Where You Find Him: In a Singles Bar.

How to Spot Him: Unfortunately you don't
until it's too late.

This man is unbelievably low. He'll be so nice to
you, that you'll think it's Christmas every day.
He'll wine you and dine you and give you such
a wonderful time that you can't believe he's
not snapped up already.
That's, of course, because he *is!*

Advantages: He's fine if you want absolutely no
commitment, and like spending weekends on your own.

Disadvantages: You'll never be sure who else he's seeing,
you only see him when he can spin a particularly good
lie . . . and your mother will never speak to you again.

MEN'S STYLE SECRETS: What to watch out for . . .

WHEN HE'S TRYING TO LOOK LIKE A BUSINESSMAN:

— Braces.
— Raincoat.
— Pinstripes.
— Boring tie.
— Mobile phone.
— Briefcase
  (Carefully locked.)

. . . TRYING TO LOOK LIKE AN ARTIST:

— Cravats.
— Floppy fringes.
— Baggy jumpers.
— Sketch pads.
— Suffering expression.
— Paint stains.
  (Carefully applied.)

. . . TRYING TO LOOK LIKE LORD OF THE MANOR:

— Tweeds.
— Wax jackets.
— Corduroys.
— Wellies.
— Range Rover.
  (Carefully splashed with mud.)

. . . TRYING TO LOOK LIKE HE'S IN A BAND:

— Long, messy hair.
— Leather jacket.
— Leather trousers.
— Roll-ups.
— B.O.
— Moody face.
  (Carefully practised.)

WHEN HE'S TRYING TO LOOK RICH:

— Cambridge T-shirts.

— Eton tie.

— Tousled hair.

— Tuxedo with white scarf.

— Bulging wallet.
(Carefully hidden.)

. . . TRYING TO LOOK LIKE A STUD:

— Tight jeans.

— Cowboy boots.

— T-shirts with rolled up sleeves

— Fake tan.

— Body hair.
(Carefully displayed.)

WHEN HE'S A BIT UNSTABLE:

Watch out for . . .

— Trousers that stop above the ankle.

— Ill-fitting anoraks.

— Teeth grinding.

— Mixing sky blue with brown.

— Excessive crimplene.

. . . WHEN HE'S A *LOT* UNSTABLE:

Watch out for . . .

— Wild eyes.

— Excessive twitching and/or dribbling.

— Tattoos across the neck.

— Him following you home.

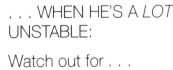

LEATHER JACKETS:

— Can be a symbol of sex and danger.

— Can make them look rich and successful.

— Can often hide a wimp in wolf's clothing.

BEARDS:

— Are a handy place to store their crumbs.

— Are worn in a 'goatie' style when they try to look artistic.

— Are shaped to hide vast, flapping double chins.

DISAPPEARING HAIR:

— Is worn long to compensate.

— Is often swept over the head.

— Is easy to spot because the hairline is thin, frizzy, and way, way back.

MOUSTACHES:

— Make them feel older.

— Make them look shifty.

— Hide their goofy teeth.

GLASSES:

— Can make them look sensitive.

— Can make them look intelligent.

— Can be easily removed so they can't look at anyone else!

WHEN HE'S NOT ALL HE SEEMS TO BE:

Watch out for . . .

— Shoulder pads.
— Stack heels.
— Toupées.
— Padded pants.

WHEN HE'S TRYING TO IMPRESS:

Watch out for . . .

— He's in a suit.
— He's covered in aftershave.
— He's *washed!*

WHEN HE'S FEELING GUILTY:

Watch out for . . .

— Large bunch of flowers.
— Sheepish grin.
— The washing done.

WHEN HE SEEMS JUST PERFECT:

Watch out for . . .

— That 666 sign.
— A battery.
— A photo of his wife.

21

SPOT THE . . .

SHORT MAN

Where You Find Him: Oops! You tripped over him.

How To Spot Him: He's the one with the enormous chip on his shoulder.

They don't have to be like this, but short men do tend to be moody and miserable, and constantly picking fights with big tall men, just to prove that they're alive.
Given half a chance, they may well be perfectly nice chaps, if only they would stop moaning for five minutes.

Advantages: You'll always feel nice and tall.

Disadvantages: You can't say things like "Don't get short with me", you'll always be dragging him away from fights, and remember . . . Hitler was short!

. . . MAN IN A SUIT . . .

Where You Find Him: On his way to, from, or working in, an office.

How To Spot Him: He's in a suit.

Forget whatever job title he's got. This man is a full-time professional suit wearer. He wears thin grey suits in winter, and thin grey suits in summer. In fact, he tends to wear the same grey suit all the time. He tries to buy interesting ties, but they all end up being grey. He hates weekends and holidays because he hasn't got a clue what to wear.

Advantages: He doesn't squander his money on clothes.

Disadvantages: He's almost as exciting as his dress sense.

MEN AND SPORT:

Sport really does bring out the worst in a man . . . his competitive streak!

There is a strong chance that it will completely take over his personality and his life.
You find he can't be just good at sport, he has to be brilliant: and not at only one sport, at *everything!*

REASONS FOR PLAYING SPORTS: To keep healthy, live longer, and to develop a sense of sportsmanship . . .

REASONS FOR JOINING SPORTS CLUBS . . .

— To get fit.
— To get out of the house.
— To extend their social life and meet new people.

... and also because we might pick up an AEROBICS TEACHER!

Men like different sports for different reasons. Some like powerful, manly sports like boxing and rugby, because they then feel powerful and manly. Especially when there's a degree of risk and disfigurement involved, and the added glee that they can easily beat *us,* if we should ever dare to challenge them.

Others prefer sports that stretch their particular skills, like darts, archery, or snooker. Sports which, incidentally, women could play against them as equal opponents. (But don't.)

Some men don't feel they can fully perform unless they're in all the right gear . . .

. . . some don't bother about the clothes but concentrate on having flashy equipment . . .

. . . and others are under the impression that because they put on a tracksuit, they are a sportsman!

SPOT THE . . .
PUBLIC SCHOOL BOY

Where You Find Him: At the cashpoint.

How To Spot Him: He's the one in the cravat with all that money.

This chap thinks he's Bertie Wooster. He goes to Hunt Balls in the evenings, and his days are planned around lying in bed and working out the best ways to spend Daddy's money.

Advantages: He'll shower you with lavish gifts and drive you around in flash cars.

Disadvantages: When it comes to sex, remember his tradition in discipline, and work out if the amount of money he spends on you is worth the embarrassment of dressing up like Nanny and beating him on the bottom with his bank book.

. . . SUPERSTUD . . .

Where You Find Him: Don't worry, he'll find YOU!

How To Spot Him: His tongue will be hanging out.

This man doesn't believe in messing about. He'll expect sex at least once on the first date or else, he says, he'll have stomach ache all night and his pants will explode.

Advantages: You may find he uses his bravado to hide the fact that he's shy, insecure, and waiting for the love of a good woman. But I doubt it.

Disadvantages: You never know where he's been, he could be riddled with all sorts of diseases, and if you don't come up with the goods on demand, he'll soon find someone who will!

This way to PARADISE!

MEN AND FOOTBALL!

I didn't include football in the sports section because to men it is not just a sport. To men football is a RELIGION!

33

Every football supporter thinks he is a better manager, player and commentator than anyone currently employed in the job . . . and they don't mind telling you so . . .

Men drive us mad about football from the day they kick their first ball. They give their opinion on every pre-match build up, shout running commentaries the minute the game is in play, criticise every decision and repeat themselves more times than *The Sound of Music*. They insist on sharing every comment and criticism with us, and wonder why it bores us to death!

There are women, however, who go to watch their partner's favourite team on Saturdays, and on Sundays they stand in the freezing cold watching them play in amateur games . . .

So Mick came hurlin' down the inside left, past two defenders, perfect ball control, straight into the penalty area, easy as you like and WHAM! Straight in the back of the net . . .

. . . then spend the rest of the weekend in a pub listening to them go over that and every other match they've ever played, in glorious detail. Why?

WHY? Because otherwise the only contact they ever have with their partners is when they get to wash their KIT!

A BRIEF LOOK AT FOOTBALLERS:

— They're what every young boy wants to grow up to be.

— They go out with Dolly Birds.

— They say things like *"The lads done well"* and *"It were a great team effort."*

— They have truly *awful* haircuts.

— They swap shirts and have baths with other men.

— They wear shiny suits in gaudy colours.

— They eventually become football managers, own fish and chip shops, or are sad old alcoholics.

— They think for a few years that they are God.

— And they're supposed to be the epitome of physical perfection and machismo . . . . . . until someone tackles them.

I WANT ME MAM.

BAD POINTS ABOUT MEN AND FOOTBALL:

— They bore you rigid.
— They encourage other men into your home to bore you rigid.
— They become obsessive, violent, childish . . . and they bore you rigid.
— They have absolutely no idea that you could possibly be bored by football, and so carry right on doing it!

GOOD POINTS ABOUT MEN AND FOOTBALL:

. . . Er . . .

. . . It gets them out of the house every Saturday . . .

SPOT THE . . .

FEMINIST MAN

Where To Find Him: He'll be close by your side.

How To Spot Him: He looks like he really, really cares.

At last you've found him! Someone who stares deep into your eyes and looks as if he really understands you. He'd never try and chat you up because he wouldn't insult your intelligence or risk ruining your deep friendship. Or so he says. In reality when he's staring intensely at you, he's trying to work out the best way to get you drunk, and the quickest way to get your bra off.

Advantages: You can pour your heart out about every Slimeball you've ever met, and he'll listen intensely.

Disadvantages: He's just another Slimeball.

. . . ARMY MAN . . .

Where You Find Him: In a gun shop.

How To Spot Him: He looks very, very unstable.

There are many reasons why men join the army. Some do it to prove they're real men, some want to be Rambo, some can't make friends and haven't got a girlfriend, some just can't get another job, and others can't exist unless someone shouts at them all day.

Advantages: They're all right if you like strict disciplinarians with hardly any hair.

Disadvantages: If he gets fed up with being shouted at, he'll start shouting at you, he insists on wearing his combat gear to bed in case war breaks out, and oh, . . . he might actually have to go to WAR!

MEN and MATING:

Men say that picking up women is *so* hard these days. (Shame!) They daren't rely on roguish charm and ask us outright in case we laugh in their face, and they can't chase after us with an impulsive bunch of flowers, in case we call the police.

HOW THEY ATTRACT OUR ATTENTION

— Whistling, grunting or groping.

— Corny old predictable chat-up lines.

— They rub up against us in lifts, stockrooms and on trains.

— They hang around in groups and shout "Gi's a smile!"

— They follow us, call out to us and hassle us so much that we *have* to look at them!

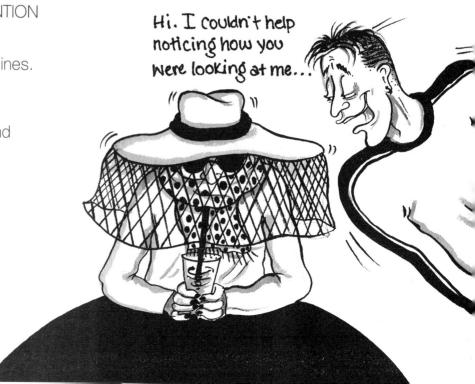

Failing that, they attempt to interpret our body language. Considering that their knowledge is gained from reading tabloids and trusting their natural instincts, it's not surprising they always mis-read ours.

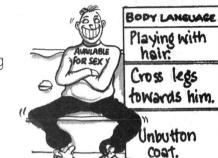

BODY LANGUAGE	WE THINK	THEY THINK
Playing with hair.	God, my hair's a mess.	She really fancies me.
Cross legs towards him.	OW! My leg's gone dead.	I'm in there...
Unbutton coat.	It's really hot in here.	WA-HEY!

The most disturbing aspect of men's mating rituals is their predictability. They always make so much effort, look as if they really mean it . . . . . . and then do EXACTLY the same with the next female they meet!

HOW TO SPOT A SINGLE MAN:

Single men are everywhere. You just have to know where to find them and what to look out for. (Just looking desperate doesn't count.)

At the supermarket: He has "Meals For One", a basket instead of a trolley, and it'll be loaded with cans of beer, pasties and crisps.

In cafés: They have loads of papers to read, order breakfast and look lonely. It could just be a ruse to get you to feel sorry for them and offer to do all their cooking.

In launderettes: Good places to start conversations and at least it shows they know how to wash. Keep an eye out for stray bras.

In record shops: They can always be found here at weekends and Bank Holidays, because without us they have no life.

TYPES OF SINGLE MEN:

THOSE WHO ARE
BETWEEN PARTNERS . . .

— Aren't looking for one.
— Are very happy with
their independence.
— Are *very* hard to catch.

THOSE WHO HAVE NEVER
HAD ONE . . .

— Are very nervous when
they're around women.
— Are not a good catch.

THOSE WHO HAVE JUST
DIVORCED ONE . . .

— Normally need care
and attention.
— Would settle for a
young nubile
sex pot.
— Normally
come
complete
with
children.

FREE!

THOSE LOOKING FOR
A ONE NIGHT STAND . . .

— Are everywhere.
— Are waiting for
you to get drunk.
— Are easy to
spot, as they
always look
far too keen.

I'M
YOURS!

. . . AND THOSE
HUNTING FOR A WIFE
AND MOTHER . . .

— Need to be
kept well clear
of!

CHECK
LIST

HOW TO CATCH ONE:

Despite the fact that most men are absolutely desperate for sex, some still have to be hit over the head with a mallet before they think about noticing you.

HE DOESN'T NOTICE YOU BECAUSE . . .

— He's not interested.
— He's involved.
— He's gay.
— He's shortsighted.

HOW TO GET HIM TO NOTICE YOU .

— Catch his eye and smile every time you see him.
— Never look desperate.
— Find out where he works, arrive as he's heading for home, and drop your shopping in his path.

  — If he doesn't start talking, get the mallet out.
  — If that doesn't work, get the hint and look for someone else.

Once you have his attention, you then have to make sure you keep it . . .

— Always look interested in him, but also as if there's something better you should be doing.
— Never look like you *will* have sex, but look as if you *might*.
— Almost touch him when you talk, but not quite. It'll drive him mad.
— Try old-fashioned flattery. But only when absolutely necessary.
— Flirt madly with someone else, preferably someone he can't stand.
— Look independent, content and perfectly happy without a man. You'll be *swamped!*

HOW TO CATCH A RICH MAN:

If you've tried hunting for true love and failed miserably, try catching a rich man instead. It might not be the love of your life . . . but who cares

— Buy a couple of classy looking outfits so you don't *look* like you're after his money.
— Hang around where you know there'll be rich men. (Polo matches, posh hotels, exclusive restaurants . . . Buckingham Palace . . .)
— Take your time and select a shortlist of hopefuls.
— Faint in front of one. Right in front. (Practise looking gorgeous whilst unconscious.)
— Or find a novel way to strike up a conversation and find out where he lives.
— If all else fails, crash into his car. He can't help but notice you then.

HOW TO TELL IF HE'S ALL FLASH AND NO CASH:

The *last* thing you want when you've set your heart on a rich man is to land one who's as broke as you are.

WATCH OUT FOR:

— Car Hire stickers on his Mercedes.
— Faded and worn patches on his Armani suits.
— Old worn out shoes.
— Fake tan that stops at his neck.
— Outward signs of wealth (Gucci T-shirts, fake Rolex watches, BMW key rings etc).
— Far too much gold jewellery.
— When he keeps trying to get you to tell how much *you* earn!

SPOT THE . . .

OFFICE PERVERT

Where You Find Him: By the photocopier.

How To Spot Him: He's far too close to you.

Watch out, watch out, the office perv's about! He'll lean over your desk, press against you whenever he can, and always tries to put his tongue in your mouth at the Christmas party.

If you tell him to bog off he'll call you frigid, and if you report him to your boss he'll only say you led him on.

Advantages: He comes in handy when you want to practise your shredding technique.

Disadvantages: He might end up as your boss.

. . . FOREIGN MAN . . .

Where You Find Him: Outside a foreign school, a tourist attraction or on your holidays.

How To Spot Him: He's tanned, he's well-dressed and he's *gorgeous!*

Not only does he look better than any man Britain can offer, but he also comes complete with a sexy accent. He mentally undresses you and calls you *Baby,* which you normally hate . . . but he can say "Two Returns To Clapham" and sound like a prince.

Advantages: You may spend the rest of your life in a villa somewhere hot and exotic.

Disadvantages: He may just be sowing his oats with you because he can't do it with the girls at home, you may end up in a child-grabbing love triangle, or you might have clashing cultures and find he expects you to have twenty children and do exactly what he tells you!

MEN and KISSING . . .

In old Hollywood movies, once a man had kissed you it was automatically assumed that you could call each other *darling* and start making wedding plans.

The kisses were long, meaningful and passionate. You never ended up with parts of his lunch in your mouth, and it was the kind of love that never smudged your lipstick . . . worlds apart from the real thing.

THE FIRST TIME KISSER:

Doesn't know what he's doing or where he's going, so he pokes your eye out whilst giving your nose a passionate snog.

THE HALITOSIS KISSER:

Never gets a second chance, so he holds you far too tight, so you can't get away.

THE EAR KISSER:

He's either been reading too many sex manuals, or else he really doesn't know where your mouth is.

THE HOOVER KISSER:

More suction power than an industrial hoover, this man is a hunk of passion. It sounds jolly nice, but stop as soon as you feel your liver in your mouth.

THE MESSY KISSER:

Your hair's messed up, your lipstick's all over your face, but you'll never need a toothpick again!

HOW TO SPOT A RAT! . . .

We will all probably encounter
at least one Rat in our lifetime.
Someone who promises the earth,
leads us a fine old dance and
messes up our lives completely
before giving us the big heave-ho
and running off with our best friend.

WHEN HE'S A MARRIED OR INVOLVED RAT:

— He never gives you his home number.
— He often cancels at the last minute.
— He hardly ever sees you at the weekends.
— He makes sudden arrangements and changes.
— He rarely sees you in daylight.
— He always takes you to quiet places where nobody will know him.
— He never stays overnight.

WHEN HE'S A
NO-COMMITMENT RAT:

— He won't commit himself to
  anything, so he can't be blamed
  for anything.

— He shares a flat with loads of other
  men, who hang around the bathroom
  to catch a glimpse of you naked.

— He has porno mags under his bed,
  as those girls make no demands of him.

— Just because he has sex with you
  doesn't mean he's committed to you.

— Just because he makes an arrangement
  to meet you, doesn't mean he'll turn up.

WHEN HE'S JUST A BIG FAT RAT:

— He never rings when he says he will.

— He never turns up on time and rarely turns up at all.

— When he's with you, he's always looking at other women.

— He always makes you feel that everything is your fault.

— He turns up after not contacting you for weeks, and not only expects you to be pleased to see him, but wants sex too!

— He doesn't break up with you to your face, he just expects you to get the hint. An invitation to his wedding usually does the trick.

57

HOW TO TELL WHEN YOU'VE GOT A RAT . . .

You arrange your life around waiting for the phone to ring . . .

. . . You never listen to your friends, who you've always trusted before . . .

You find yourself making excuses for him, and even when you *know* he's a rat, you secretly believe that you are the woman to change him.

If you find yourself doing any of these, get out now . . . or else you're on your own!

SPOT THE . . .

MOTHER'S BOY

Where You Find Him: Down the shops.

How To Spot Him: He's usually in beige, and has a side parting and dominated expression.

When a man is over 35 with no history of ever having any girlfriends and he still lives with his mother, he's either been working on an oil rig for most of his life . . . or there's something seriously wrong somewhere!

Advantages: You could mould him exactly how you'd like, because he'll be so grateful to have a girlfriend.

Disadvantages: I know some women like a man who's a challenge, but you'd have to play Match With Mother for the rest of your life. Also remember the most famous mother's boy was Norman Bates in Psycho!

. . . FASHION ODDITY . . .

Where You Find Him: At the dry cleaners.

How To Spot Him: He looks weird!

A few years ago he would have been called an Ugly Old Git, but thanks to wacky designer clothes, he's becoming rather a popular accessory. He'll be a hairdresser or a designer, and will probably want you to dress as badly as he does, if that's possible.

Advantages: At least you know people aren't laughing at you!

Disadvantages: His passion for fashion far outweighs anything else, and he won't want to risk crumpling his Ozbeks. Mind you, when you see him *out* of his clothes, you'll probably be grateful!

MEN and SEX . . .

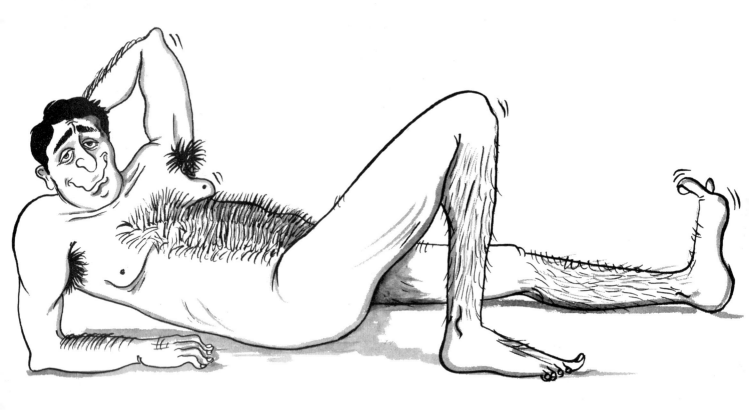

There's not an awful lot
of mystery surrounding
men when it comes to sex . . .

. . . there's no *will-he-won't-he*
time-consuming playing
hard to get for *them!*

It all starts when they're
teenagers and they have
to cope with insecurities,
lack of knowledge and
leaping hormones.
And it goes downhill
from there . . .

There are countless contradictions, endless exaggerations and loads of downright LIES regarding men and sex, mainly involving how good they are at it, how often they do it, and especially these days, how many partners they've had . . .

. . . all of which can be altered at a moment's notice, depending on which version suits them best at the time.

The main reasons why men tell so many lies are their delicate egos and their insecurities, which make them unable to talk honestly amongst themselves. When we are unsure about a relationship we talk to our friends or we read magazine articles written by other women, all who openly share their own experiences and aren't afraid to tell the truth, however embarrassing.

Where do men get their information? Other men and TABLOIDS. No wonder they have a weird, stereotyped view of women!)

A TABLOID'S VIEW OF WOMEN:
(Gawd help us!)

FEMININE WOMEN:
Easy on the eye, good in the home, always there when you fancy a quickie . . . and best of all, they know their place

SHAGABILITY: 10

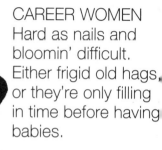

CAREER WOMEN
Hard as nails and bloomin' difficult. Either frigid old hags, or they're only filling in time before having babies.

SHAGABILITY: 2

SWEDISH WOMEN:
They may be brain surgeons or nuclear physicists . . . but to us lads they'll always mean Au Pairs and SEX!

SHAGABILITY: 10

FEMINISTS:
Blinkin' nuisances! They make our lives a misery just because they can't get a man. The author of this book probably looks like this!

SHAGABILITY: 0

GLAMOUR GIRLS:
Good for the ego, good to
be seen with, and a
guaranteed good time.
They cost too much to
keep, so dump 'em as
soon as you can.

SHAGABILITY: 10

SPORTY WOMEN:
Great bodies, really fit,
and can really wear a
man out. Avoid actually
playing any sport, as
they'll probably beat you.

SHAGABILITY: 8

FOREIGN WOMEN:
Smart, chic and sexy.
Unfortunately when
they get old, turn into
a big fat blob with a
moustache. Only have
when young.

SHAGABILITY: 6

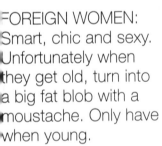

UGLY WOMEN:
Always grateful for
any attention, they're
the easiest to get into
bed, and they don't
make many demands.
Turn the lights out.

SHAGABILITY: 3

WHAT MEN WORRY ABOUT WHEN IT COMES TO SEX . . .

Men do have some insecurities, mainly that we might compare them to past boyfriends . . .

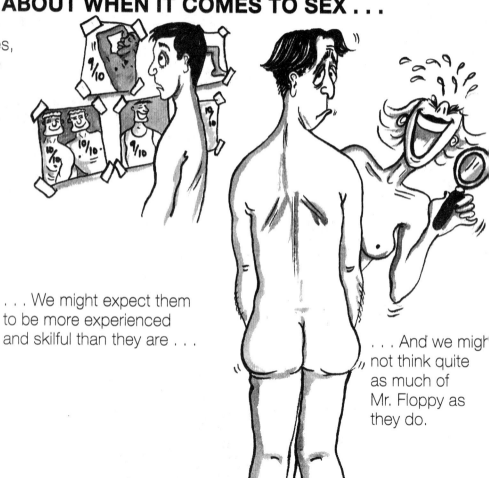

. . . We might expect them to be more experienced and skilful than they are . . .

. . . And we might not think quite as much of Mr. Floppy as they do.

WHAT IS SEXY IN A MAN?

— Broad, manly shoulders.

— Twinkling eyes.

— Nice firm bum.

— His own teeth.

— Good legs.

— Not too many muscles.
(But enough.)

— Personal hygiene.

— Oh . . . a nice personality
and a sense of humour.

(. . . Now I need a cold shower . . .)

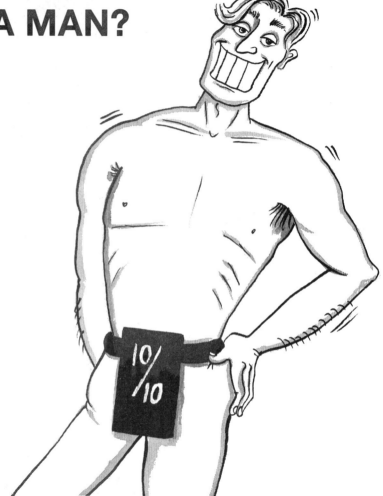

. . . AND WHAT ISN'T?

— Ginger hair.

— Pot bellies.

— Flabby bums.
(Girls don't make passes
at men with big . . .)

— Dandruff.

— Hairy backs.

— Nose and ear hair.

— Constant scratching.

— B.O.

— When he has a bigger bust than you.

— Looking like they need a cook, a
cleaner and a maid.

— Looking too desperate.

(. . . *Now I need a* SICK BAG . . .)

SPOT THE . . .

BORING MAN

Where You Find Him: Everywhere!

How To Spot Him: He's very, very boring.

These men bore you to death about anything they feel they know best about, which is *everything!* They can't talk about their cars without reciting the entire manual, they read insurance policies out loud to their children and they can talk for hours about motorway routes, house extensions, drum solos and, of course, football.

Advantages: You'll never need sleeping pills.

Disadvantages: They're dull, they have no sense of humour and they're boring, boring, BORING!

.. SENSITIVE MAN . . .

Where You Find Him: At the Bottle Bank.

How To Spot Him: He's in some form of knitwear.

He's thoughtful, he's interesting, he objects to pornography, he cares about the environment and is dedicated to finding your G-spot. Unfortunately he's also about as sexy as a damp dishcloth.

Advantages: He's a darned good friend, he listens to your problems and will always feed your cat when you're on holiday with someone sexier.

Disadvantages: He's into all things natural, so if you did get desperate and married him, he'd expect at least ten children, born without unnatural painkillers. Don't even think about it.

MEN AND THEIR PANTS:

WHY ARE MEN UNFAITHFUL?

It's a well-known fact that men are ruled by the activities going on in their pants. Their minds and their mouths may be rational, intelligent and sensitive, but you can guarantee something totally different is happening in their pants.

There are many myths (and excuses) surrounding male sexuality and the reason why they stray, most of which were started decades ago and were passed on by parents and grandparents who unfortunately *believed* them!

WHAT TO DO ABOUT IT . . .

There are many places you can turn to for advice.

Your friends tell you to give him up . . .

Tabloids tell you to dress up like a tart to keep him . . .

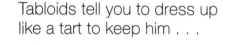

. . . and as for your MOTHER . . .

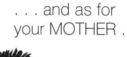

or you could confront him yourself . . .

As usual, the excuses come out when men are put on the spot. The favourites are *"She didn't mean anything . . ."* *"Men have a menopause too"* . . . and *"I wanted to find myself"* . . .

WHY DO WOMEN TAKE IT SO BADLY?

. . . Because he never made any effort for you . . .

Don't wanna go anywhere Don't wanna do anything.

TV BITS

. . . He gave you the slobbiest years of his life . . .

. . . and anyway, you turned down the chance of a really nice fling, out of LOYALTY!!

. . . He might have given you all kinds of infections . . .

You are requested at the clinic for a CHECK UP RIGHT NOW!

Run Away With Me...

SPOT THE EXCUSES . . .

When he never does any housework . . .

. . . When he doesn't come home at all!

. . . When he doesn't pay any maintenance . . .

. . . When he comes home late . . . AGAIN!

it didn't mean anything...
I was too drunk to stop....
...Suddenly we were in BED....
...I don't know HOW it happened...
...I didn't like to say no....
...It'll NEVER happen again...
...I didn't know what I was doing...
....It was just a PHASE I was going through.......

NEW MEN:

Poor loves. So confused! Desperate to twang our bra straps and peek down our blouses, but knowing that they have to appreciate us as equals first.

They won't treat a woman as if she was a Bozo, they won't automatically assume that her greatest job in life is to bear their children . . . and giving her a quick smack in the mouth would never cross their minds!

They have decent haircuts.

They look after their bodies.

They WASH!

They're not afraid to wear pastels or patterns.

They can do their own washing and ironing.

They're sensitive lovers.

They read intelligent men's magazines. (That only have artistic photos of naked women.)

. . . and they can talk for hours without even mentioning FOOTBALL!

M'SIEUR

But unfortunately there are drawbacks with New Men. Some have had to battle so hard against the Neanderthal inside that they've forgotten that we like a bit of a caveman now and again. In extreme cases you find you can't have a good row because he always sees your point of view, and you can't have a quick bonk without him turning it into a seven hour performance.

Others become over sensitive and over serious, and end up being deeply unsexy. On top of that they have no sense of fun, and their sense of humour disappears without trace. It's almost enough to send us screaming to the nearest building site. (But not quite.)

SEE NO HUMOUR **HEAR NO HUMOUR** **TELL NO JOKES**

...WHERE'S MY DINNER?

Mind you, we shouldn't really complain, because we don't know how soon the novelty will wear off and we'll be back to the Bad Old Days before you can say Bernard Manning . . .

SPOT THE . . .

REAL MAN

Where You Find Him: In a pub, on a street corner, a building site or down a hole in the road.

How To Spot Him: His bottom is hanging out.

He's unsightly, unhygienic, has a pot belly and he *still* thinks you fancy him! He thinks that Women's Rights are just the opposite to women's lefts, and that foreplay is when you take your socks off.

Advantages: Can't think of any.

Disadvantages: He believes that big boys don't cry, they just bottle it all up and take it out on you later, he subscribes to *Playthings* every month, he thinks that B.O. is a turn-on . . . . . . and yet he always manages to find someone to marry him. Why?

. . PETER PAN MAN . . .

Where You Find Him: Reading comics in a newsagents.

How To Spot Him: He can't stop fidgeting.

Erratic and hyperactive, he wears T-shirts with farty slogans and brightly coloured clothes. He acts younger than he is and looks younger than he is, until he starts to go bald, and then he just looks creepy.

Advantages: He's lively, entertaining and will make you feel young as long as you can keep up with him.

Disadvantages: He's not likely to settle down until he's eighty, and if he does sit still long enough to get down to sex, it'll be like going to bed with the little boy next door.

NEW FATHERS . . .

Wouldn't you know it, men have discovered parenthood! They've only taken a few thousand years to realise it takes two to tango, that babies are not made by women alone, and that they really should be doing half of the work . . .

Convenient, isn't it, that they waited until the age of the automatic washing machine, disposable nappies, instant food and microwaves, before they joined in!!

THEN . . . .   **NOW . . . .**

The main reason for this sudden surge in male interest has to be the arrival of ADVERT MAN on our televisions. They quite like the art director's idea of fatherhood; muscles, suntans, two cars, a quiet baby and all the hair gel they could ever need . . .

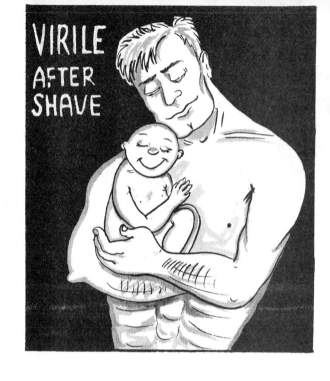

REAL MAN RAZORS
- HEY, YOU'RE *FERTILE!*

. . . . The families are always happy, they never get woken up through the night, but most of all, they're all *beautiful!*

. . So now the New Man we had looked forward to for so long, who loved our independent minds and stretch mark-free stomachs has suddenly decided that he likes the look of fatherhood. He now starts talking about body clocks and designer buggies, and does his best to get us pregnant.

Not only are New Fathers very keen on the prospect of fatherhood, they are now also EXPERTS.
To prove this, we are inundated with them, appearing on television, radio, writing books and passing on their invaluable knowledge.
(See? They even have time to do all THAT).

But will we ever see New Fathers taking their new found experience and enlightenment into the workplace?

95

New Fathers also want to share as much of the pregnancy as possible. They share your anti-natal classes, they share your dismay at trying to find something decent to wear, they share the joys of watching films of other births whilst trying hard not to be sick. The one experience they never offer to share with you is the PAIN!

There are advantages to New Fathers.
Whilst it's all still new and interesting
they do their share, they enable you to
have time to yourself and if it lasts,
you can have a happy and equal
life as parents.

(Now all we've got to do is work out
a way to get them PREGNANT!)

SPOT THE . . .

D.I.Y. MAN

Where You Find Him: Up a ladder.

How To Spot Him: He's constantly looking for something to tinker with.

Don't ever marry one of these! You spend half your life up to your armpits in rubble, and the other half waiting for the shelves to fall down and the conservatory to collapse.

Advantages: You always know where he is, and you never have to pay for tradesmen. (Unless it all goes horribly wrong.)

Disadvantages: He never wants to go out, because he's got that grouting to do, and if you do manage to get him out, he turns into Boring Man because he's got nothing else to talk about. Get him to build a big shed in the garden, and move him in!

. . . BEAUTIFUL MAN . . .

Where You Find Him: Anywhere with lots of mirrors.

How To Spot Him: He's staring at himself.

This man either is a model, or wants everyone to think he is. He's very, very good looking. So much so that you want to paint a couple of spots on his face to break the monotony.

Advantages: He's jolly nice to look at.

Disadvantages: He pinches all your moisturiser, he won't have a good laugh in case he gets wrinkles, he won't get down to raunchy sex in case it messes his hair up, and if he thinks you look better than he does, he won't leave the house.

GAY MEN . . .

It's a great disappointment to red-blooded heterosexual females that a large number of handsome, well-groomed and interesting men aren't going to be interested in them . . . EVER!

Unless he fits a typical gay stereotype, a girl usually can't tell a man is gay until she's got him pinned up against a wall and finds he's *not* snogging back. In this situation, what can you do?
(. . . Ask if he's got a brother!)

One thing worse than finding the man of your dreams is gay, must be finding the man you live with, in one of your dresses! (Especially if he looks better in it than you do.) What can you do?
(. . . Lock up your wardrobe!)

(GAY)

(NOT GAY)
(HELP!)

MEN at WORK . . .

You learn a great deal about men when you have to work with them all day. Firstly you discover that they become very territorial, and are constantly asserting their personal space and invading yours!

. . Then you discover that they have an awful lot of undesirable habits, and you're working in the living world of scratch n' sniff . . .

. . Heh . . . heh . . . Halitosis . . .

. . . Hair trimming . . . . . . and, of course, Harassment!

103

. . . You also find you become an expert at spotting men on the threshold of the male menopause; decision-makers, politicians and world leaders with our lives in their hands, who turn into gibbering wrecks whose only solace for their insecurities is to run off with a brainless bimbo!

SPOT THE . . .

MAN IN A CAR

Put a man in a car
and his true personality
comes to light . . .

MAN IN A VAN:
Crashability: 10

He doesn't let his
driving interfere
with his leering.

PSYCHO-CARDIAC MAN:
Crashability: 10

MOBILE MAN: Crashability: 10

. . . Doesn't let his driving interfere with
his business deals.

. . . Doesn't let his driving interfere with
his vendetta against the world.

...orget the old idea about
...e type of cars reflecting
...e size of a man's trousers . . .
. . . did you know that how
...ey drive will show you
...ow they'll be in bed?

MR. STEADY and RELIABLE:

No good if you crave adventure,
as he doesn't take any risks.
You may think he's a little
bit dull, but at least you
know he'll do it properly.

MR. SPEED KING:

...oesn't use a seat belt, never takes
...recautions, he likes to have a thrilling
...de . . . but the journey's always over
...efore you know it.

MR. CAUTIOUS:

PHUT!

. . . Takes a long time to get going, worries
far too much about making a mistake,
dribbles along far too slowly . . . and
then conks out altogether.

MEN and OLD AGE:

What are men like when they get old?
They dribble, they smell, they have no control over their bodily functions, and they sit around all day doing nothing and talking rubbish. (No change there, then!)

OLD MEN WEAR:

Zip up jackets
Sleeveless pullovers
Dew drops
Bri-nylon shirts
Ear hair
Scarves
Slacks
Cardigans
Brylcreem
Grey or beige
Bad toupées
Old Spice
Their medals.

And what about New Men? What will they be like when they're old men? Will they have face-lifts and liposuction? Will they be sprightly partners who are fit and active, who wear good clothes and retire with us to sunnier climes?

OLD NEW MEN WILL WEAR:

Armani
Hair gel
Hair dye
Silk
Chinos
Ray Bans
Moisturiser
Donor cards

. . . or will we be forever stuck with men who wear the same clothes until they die (with the same stain down the front), who discuss their bowel movements whenever possible, who think that we retire so we can look after them . . . and who live in hope that because they can make babies until they're ninety, that some young girl will actually *want* them to?

HAS YOUR MAN FULLY EVOLVED?

ARE YOU LIVING WITH A NEW MAN OR A NEANDERTHAL? FIND OUT NOW!

1 A young, slim blonde Babe wiggles past.
DOES HE:

a Push you to one side and chase after her, shouting *"So long, FATSO?"*
b Start to dribble, but hides it well?
c Not even notice her, as he only has eyes for you?

2 You want him to go with you on an all day shopping trip; his idea of Hell.
DOES HE:

a Staple himself to the sofa and refuse to budge?
b Agree to go, only if you go with him in all the record shops?
c Jump up, grab his cheque book and get the car out?

3 He's started reading Mothercare catalogues. You say you don't want children until you're good and ready . . . if at all.
DOES HE:

a Call you a Lesbian and run off with your best friend?
b Fully understand, but still gazes wistfully at Pampers ads?
c Offer to have a baby himself?

4 A tall, bronzed muscular hunk walks past.
DOES HE:

a Try to find a way to pick a fight?
b Suck in his stomach and make a joke about overcooked meat?
c Start to cry?

5 Your all-time favourite film coincides with the Cup Final, and the video is broken.
DOES HE:

a Laugh in your face, invite all his mates round AND expect you to feed them?
b Go to a friend's house to watch the match?
c Say it's not as important as you are, and watches the film with you?

6 You get a spanking new job or promotion, which means you now earn more than he does.
DOES HE:

a Have an affair to re-affirm his masculinity?
b Throw you a party?
c Start to cry?

7 You're not having sex as much as you used to.
DOES HE:
• Say there's nothing wrong with him and has an affair?
• Arrive home dressed as Tarzan, promising a night of Hot Jungle Lovin'?
• Get out the 48 hour *Love Discovery* Videos?

8 You're going away for the weekend, and ask a simple question regarding the route you'll take.
DOES HE:
• Say *"I know where I'm going"* and then shout at you when he gets lost?
• Explain in less than 50 words?
• Get out the atlas, the compass, the calculator, and explains every B-road, every turn; *and* what's on the menu at the motorway café?

9 *The Sport* has a graphic centrefold feature on "SINDY WITH THE SIXTY-INCH SIZZLERS."
DOES HE:
a Believe it, go a bit wobbly, and put the picture over your bed?
b Laugh?
c Get deeply offended and complain to the Press Council?

10 You have a job as well as a young baby, and ask for a bit more help around the house.
DOES HE:
a Change one nappy a month and say you should be grateful?
b Get deeply ashamed and do extra shifts at night feeding?
c Offer to give up his job and become a House Husband?

NOW SEE THE RESULTS. . .

RESULTS

MOSTLY A Have you noticed any excessive body hair? Does he have a liking for raw meat? Does he try to test your hair for dragability? Because you have chosen a real live CAVEMAN! *WHY? WHY? WHY?*

MOSTLY B He doesn't sound too bad at all. Men like this should not only be snapped up, but preserved for posterity. Get him pickled in vinegar quick, before he changes his mind.

MOSTLY C Oh dear. What a SAP! He means well, I know, but he's a bit of a doormat, isn't he? If you like them submissive, fine . . . but otherwise inject some *hormones* or something!

A FINAL THOUGHT . . . .
Did you know that we choose a partner who looks
like us, who has a similar build and face shape; who
likes what we like, hates what we hate, and laughs
at what makes us laugh?
In short, someone who is JUST LIKE US! . . . .